Black Girl Shine

—

Aissatou Bah

ISBN: 978-1-9995538-1-4

Illustrations by Rabiatou Bah
soulababe.com
@soula.rb

Edited by Ann Marie Collymore

Electronically issued in Canada

aissatou.tbah@gmail.com

www.aissatoubah.com

@aissatoutb

For my beautiful Black girls and Queens.

For my beautiful Black boys and Kings.

To the people reading this book—I appreciate you.

Thank you. Never stop shining.

index.

BLACK GIRL MAGIC

Aissatou Bah

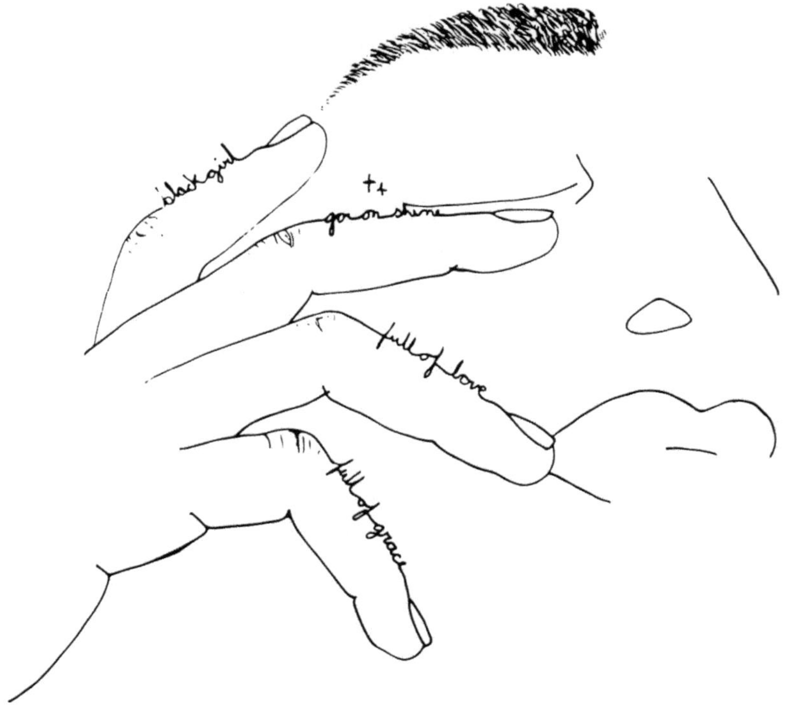

'Black Girl Shine'

Ringlets and curls,
Elastic and swirls,
Black girl, go on shine!
Smooth skin,
Lips, full of love within,
Black girl, go on shine!
Thick thighs, thin waist,
Confident, stride full of grace,
Black girl, go on shine!
Your hips carry the stories of your ancestors,
And your back arches with the strength you've inherited.
Your eyes twinkle with wisdom,
And your presence is easily pure magic,
Black girl, go on, shine!

Aissatou Bah

'Black Beauty'

Black has never been more beautiful.
They say, a spark is all it takes,
For a fire to grow,
And when that spark ignites,
It can blind you with its glow.

You're that spark,
So beautiful, inspiring others,
Who are different shades of you,
To appreciate the beauty of melanin,
Fluctuating in pigmentation and hue—

And when you're down,
Believe you will be supported,
By the many brothers and sisters,
You selflessly enheartened with energy,
A synergy, so powerful it seldom quivers,
For Black, is beautiful, beyond complexity.

Aissatou Bah

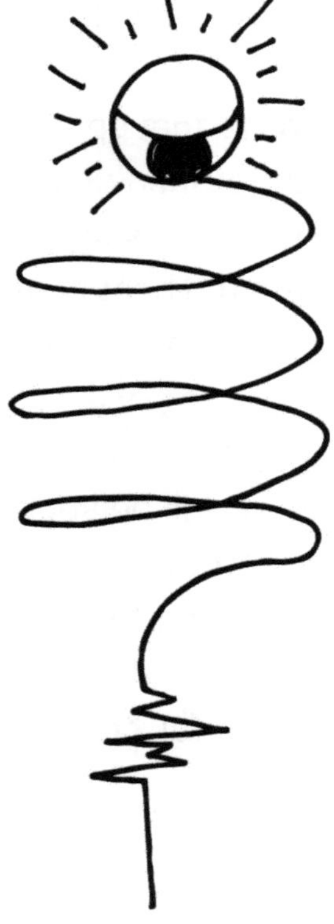

'Rise and Shine'

There's something special about the sunrise. How even when you close your eyes, you can still sense its light. You can even feel its warmth penetrate the hoods of your eyes. It's amazing how something we can't directly stare at can make us feel so alive and rejuvenated—a powerful ball of energy selflessly distributing happiness. As the days wear on, wintertime comes around, and the sun's energy falters. What if I told you, that she was simply taking time to recharge? What if I told you that even when she's gone you haven't lost anything? The sun's energy is actually inside us, carrying the light we unknowingly collect inside our hearts, and encouraging us to spread it until her return. See, there are no losses, as she embarks on a journey around the world to bless others like she has blessed us. So, cherish each and every day you are granted the privilege of opening your eyes—cherish the mornings that you are gifted with the chance to experience light. And know that her warmth will always be right there, comforting you in times of tenebrosity.

Aissatou Bah

'Butter Babe'

The sun rises at the same time as morning prayer.
The birds and flowers buzz with conversation,
Whilst the trees stretch their stiff limbs out.

As you bask in the morning's dew,
A neighbour brews dark fragrant coffee.
You take a deep breath in, and exhale—
officially beginning your morning ritual.
Stepping into the hot shower,
you gently scrub yesterday's worries away.

Eventually, you emerge from your cleanse,
Grabbing your trusty tin of shea butter.
You dip your fingers in—immediately welcoming its
smooth kisses on your skin.
Then, you ensure that a thin, but protective layer of love,
ambition and moisture is sealed within.

Dance, Butter Babe. Everything's in sync.

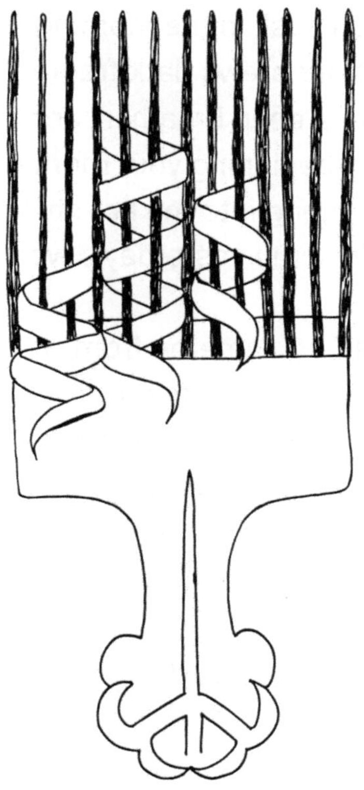

'Curl'

She says she doesn't care
About the texture of her hair
Yet she combs through it recklessly—
impatient with her tangles.

Twisting the strands at any and every angle
She sighs and hurls her comb in frustration—
Unable to find the patience to deal with such
"abomination".

After a long look into the mirror,
Things start to get a little clearer—
For the ringlets look quite happy
perched atop her head.

She giggles, a sound that soon
turns into a soft chuckle, and
Allows herself to worry about
other things instead.

Aissatou Bah

D	L	M	M	J	V	S
1	2	3	4	5	6	7
X	X	X	X	X	X	X
8	9	10	11	12	13	14
X	X	X	X	X	X	X
15	16	17	18	19	20	21
X	X	X	X	X	X	X

'Laugh'

Every day is the perfect day to
Throw that intricate head of curls back—
And laugh.

'Mane'

There's a story behind your name—
A piece of ancestry that never dies.

There's a story behind your mane—
A rich and artistic history present, but disguised.

Aissatou Bah

'Secrets'

True sisters share the secrets
Laying within their crowns.

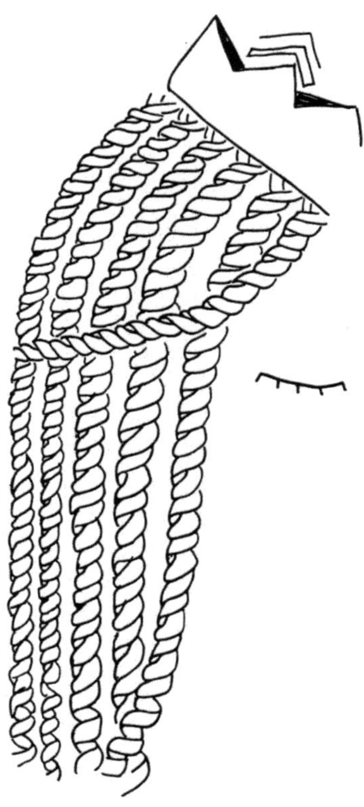

'Society'

She shined like gold,
Thick or thin,
Refusing to fit the mould,
Society wished to place her in.
Cocoa brown skin,
Thick braided locks,
And a shiny white grin,
Mixed with a voice dripping smart talk,
She did because she could,
Even if they thought her wings never would.
She rose like never before,
With the fellow colourful sisters she adores.

Aissatou Bah

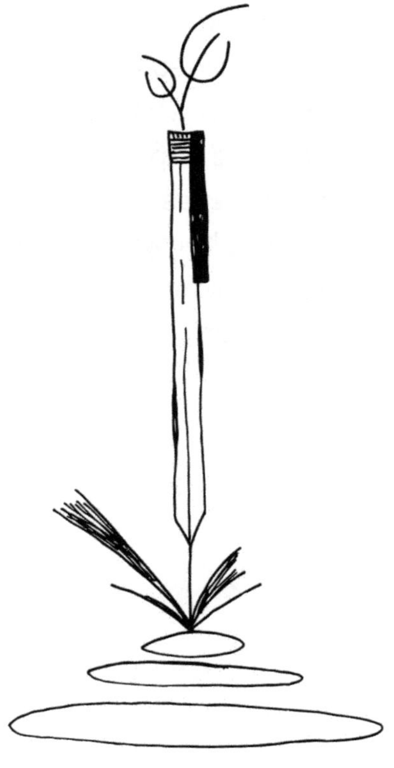

'Xiomara'

She had a voice.
In order to make use of her gift,
She picked up paper and pen,
Spilling the secrets,
Hiding deep within her soul—and then,
An amazing thing ensued.
It started as a small noise,
Slowly getting louder,
The people who listened and felt her woes,
Clapped, and could not be any prouder.

To this day,
She is an inspiration and stands tall,
Truly, the greatest masterpiece of them all.

Aissatou Bah

'Thunder'

The greatest acoustic of all time
Is the sound of thunder that forms
From the stomping of your feet,
Travelling up towards the laughter in your stomach and
Unconditional love vibrating in your heart—
Until it reaches the most electric part of you:

Your voice.

'Kenya'

Kenya smiles
Kenya sings
Kenya does not let a man clip her wings

Kenya flies
Kenya wins
Kenya does not let the fat on her body dictate things

Kenya eats
Kenya works
Kenya does not let nobody undervalue her worth

Kenya plays
Kenya strives
Kenya does not let her blessings go once they've arrived

Kenya's smart
Kenya's cool
Kenya isn't afraid to be called a fool

Aissatou Bah

'Badge'

She wears her pride
Like a badge of honour,
Even though behind that shiny shell
Hides an unbearable emotional pain.

Nonetheless, above her left breast lays
An emblem which shall always symbolize a collection of
Her combined struggles, wins and overall journey
all of which will not have gone unjustified.

'Mercury'

I now call my closest friends 'Mercury'
Because they navigate through sun waves like magnets—
Unafraid to surf on the toughest rays.

Aissatou Bah

'Explore'

There's an entire garden in her hair—
A completely unexplored ecosystem,
Waiting to be discovered.

Go unearth its beauty.

Aissatou Bah

'Jump'

Going after what your soul desires
Is the hardest and greatest thing
You could ever do, for
You remain where you are unless you take the leap—
So, jump
Your brothers and sisters will be near
To soften the blow
When you fall.

They'll also be present
When you rise again—this time,
Equipped with the strength of one who has learned
How to jump even higher.

Aissatou Bah

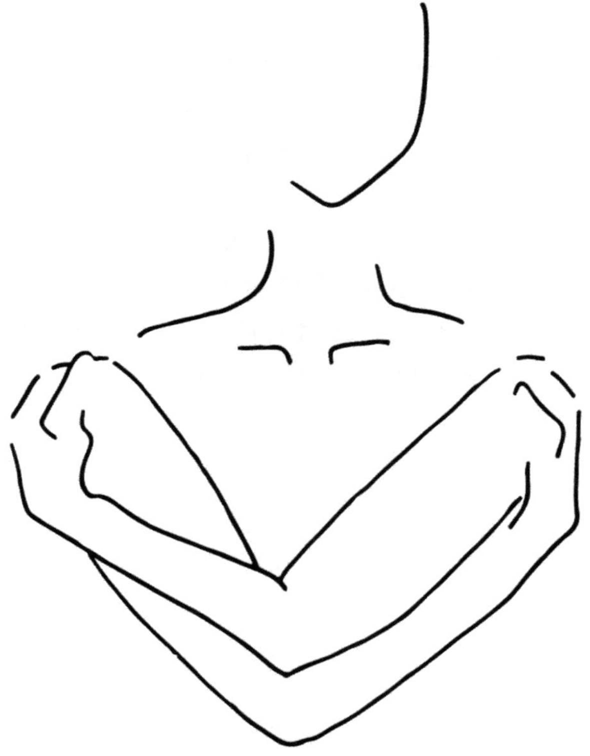

'Love Lessons'

Learn how to crave and embrace your own voice
Before craving the whispers of another.
Inhale. Exhale. And repeat after me:
"'You're important and I love you."

Aissatou Bah

'Baby Girl'

If I ever get the chance to
Welcome into this world a baby girl
I will cherish each and
Every inch of her baby curls

Her eyebrows will curve
Just like her daddy's
And she'll have lashes
Stretching upwards to meet its arches

Her nose will be as cute
As a belly button
Her pink lips
Contrasting perfectly with
Her brown skin

And I know that I'll be carrying
The most precious treasure in my arms
Because she'll grow up
Surrounded by all the support needed to accomplish
Whatever her heart desires

Aissatou Bah

'Bounty'

She was particularly ravishing
Due to the fact that
The source of her happiness
Originated from the bounty of her heart.

Aissatou Bah

'Sunset'

As the sun kisses the horizon,
The warm glow in her brown eyes
Continues to softly breathe life into you.

WE THE PEOPLE

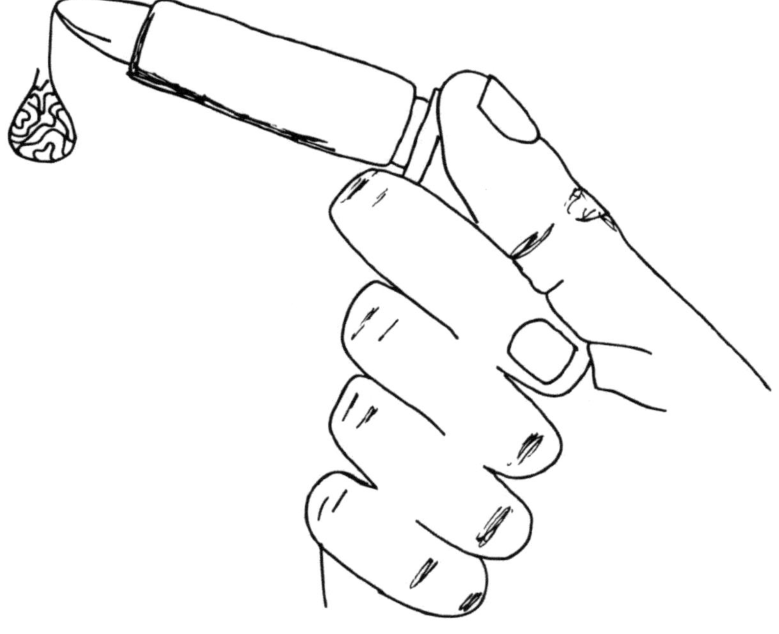

'Trigger'

Have you ever carried around
The casket of an empty gun?
Legend says that even if you manage
to reload it with bullets
Nothing will matter more
Then when your fingers contemplate
on pulling the trigger.

Aissatou Bah

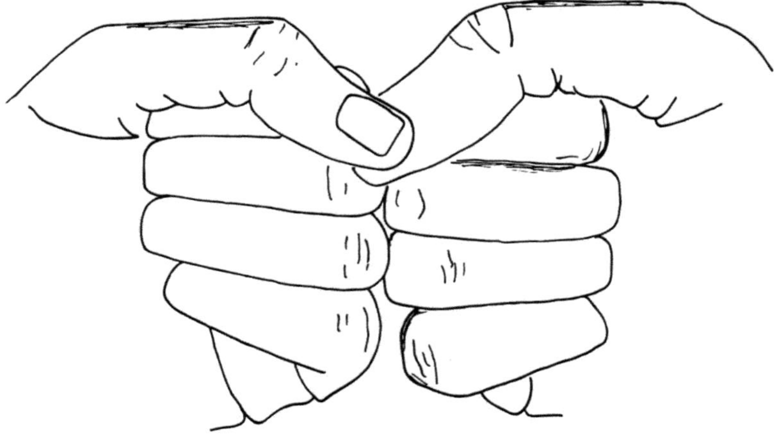

'Fear'

The fear,
Is what holds us back,

While simultaneously,
Encouraging us to attack.

All we truly need,
Is the love for our own kind,
Regardless of the skin pigmentation,
Faith, origin, sex, or state of mind.

Let us all unite, for the sake of humankind.

'Maiden'

Cotton basket
People—assets
Slain, drastic
Black casket
Tears—splashes
Purple ashes
Owner lashes
Bloody gashes
Brothers defiant
Quiet riot
Mother giant
Baby pilot
Yellow maiden
Blue haven
One life given?
Another taken.

Aissatou Bah

'Skin'

They love
To embrace lighter skin complexions
And compare
Mine to dirt, but
Little do they know
That my skin is the tree
My neck the trunk
And my hair
The beautiful
And evergreen
Foliage

Aissatou Bah

'Pigment'

They say that the ability to see colour
Is actually a pigment of the imagination.
So, I want you to visualize
A thousand butterflies
Simultaneously colliding into each other.

That—is me.

Aissatou Bah

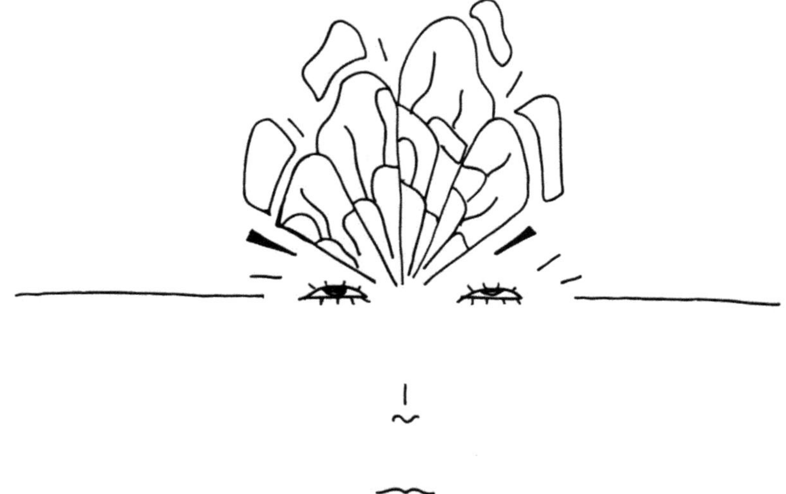

'Rise'

The truth is,
They want us to stay down.
But we shall rise.

The truth is,
They wish us to be uneducated.
But we shall rise.

Rise like the sun,
At the top of the morning,

Rise like the sea,
When the thunder is roaring,

Rise like the gun,
That points at our skin without warning,

Rise like the honey bee,
That works tirelessly to feed me—supporting,

We shall rise.

Aissatou Bah

'Ignite'

Oftentimes we allow them to
Throw ice into our fiery souls, but
Last time I checked,
A spark could still ignite a fire.

Aissatou Bah

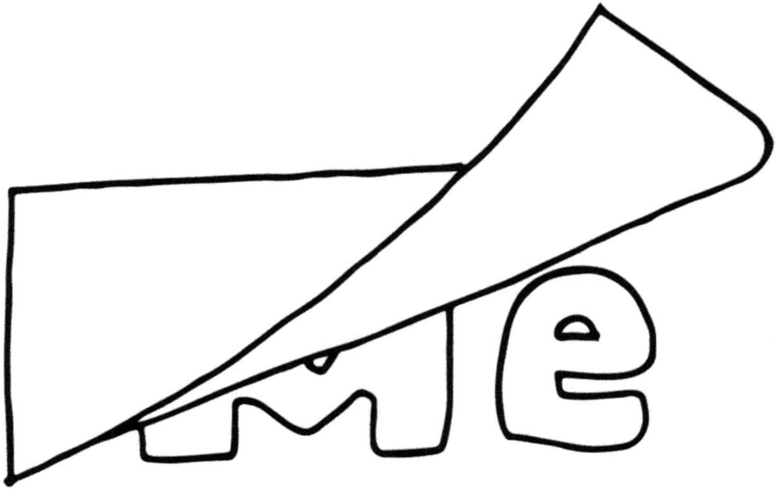

'Labels'

Labels, are in fact made to
Repel beautiful, but stubborn, ink away.

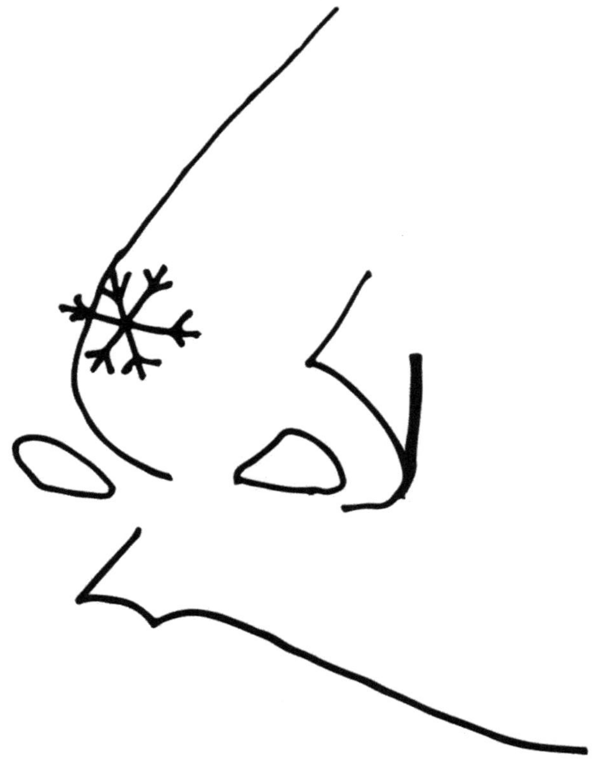

'Soul Child'

When we suppress
Our urges to create,
We hurt the most important part of our soul;
The child within.

One who once looked at the world,
Like it had found the shiniest gem, and
Giggled when snow,
Touched the tip of its nose.

That child is in you,
But weeps every day—
Every day, you forget to feed,
That sweet, soul child.

Aissatou Bah

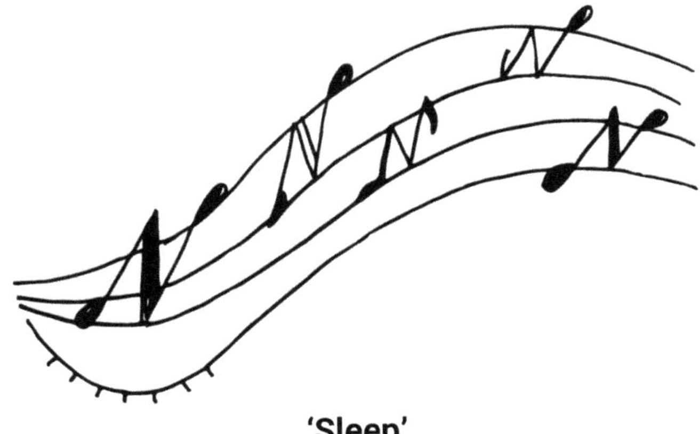

'Sleep'

Consciousness is underrated.
Every day,
People walk past you
Without realizing your worth.

This often includes strangers, friends
Family, lovers and haters.

Don't make the mistake,
Of listening to their misleading lullabies,
Laced with petty and jealous lies—

If they want to slumber on you,
Let them sleep.

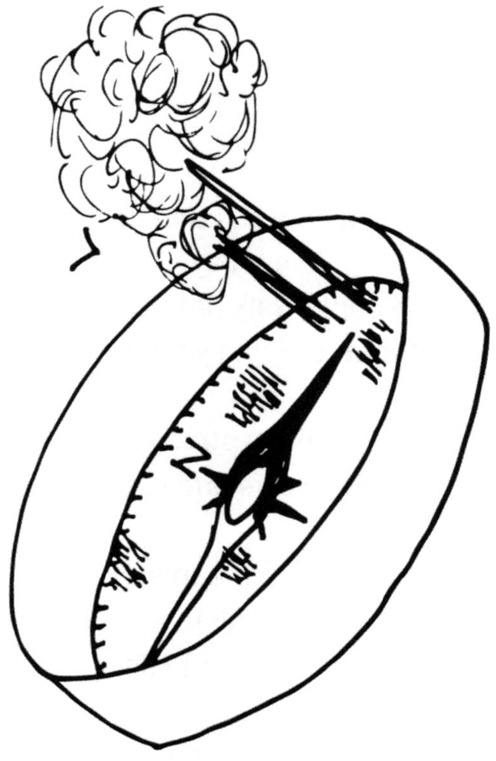

'Forest'

Ignoring your moral compass
Is like building a forest
Without maintaining its ecosystem.

First, you must allow what seems like
Tiny meaningless bugs
To neutralize the environment.

Second, secure a steady stream of water—
The income that gives
Earth its sustenance.

Thirdly, cultivate a nutritious earth,
Otherwise, the plans you hope to grow
Will never take root.

Lastly, without the fire and drive of passion,
You will block
Your chances at rebirth.

Planning for the path ahead is turning
your resources into bread.

'Mirage'

Fogginess removed
Doubt becomes an illusion,
And you, even stronger than its mirage.

Aissatou Bah

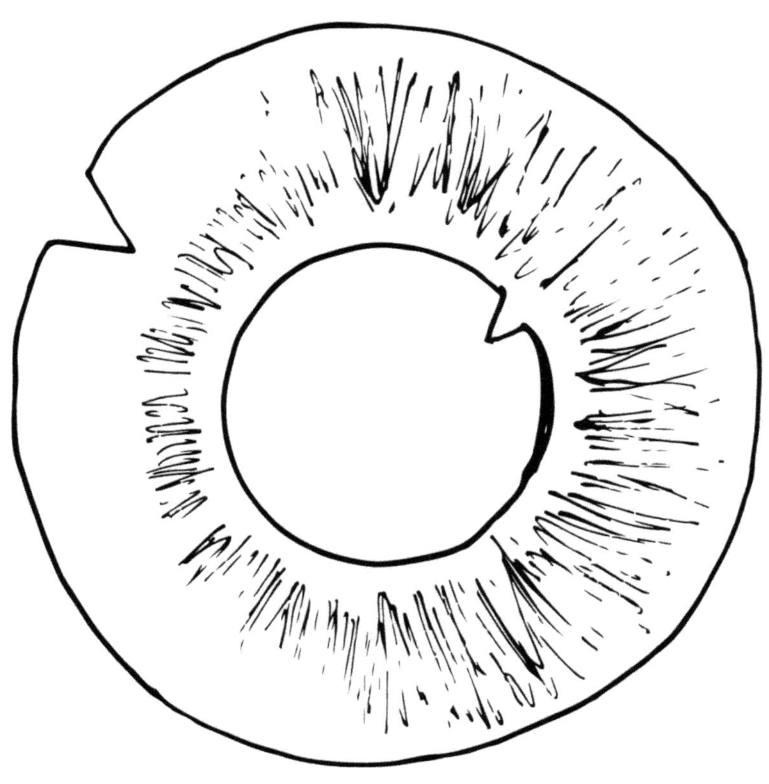

'In the Eyes of the Beholder'

I can see it in your eyes—
All of life's burns,
The hurt, anger and pain,
The detours and wrong turns.

It's important that you know that
After every tragedy your irises have perceived,
You still have the ability to turn
every dull image into beauty.

Aissatou Bah

'Tears'

Tears will be shed both in the morn and eve—
All because of the broken promises,
Unattained goals, and
Fruitless declarations of change.

But when all the salt has been shed,
You'll be left with a bright lamp for the future.

Aissatou Bah

'Soil'

Her tears soiled the brittle earth
Beneath the soles of her feet,
Feeding the roots of success
She did not know would eventually reach her.

Each morning, when the sun would rise,
She would keep her head up,
Blessing the butterflies in her garden
With her scintillating smile.

However, at night,
Her sorrows would drown the worms,
Who in turn writhed helplessly
In a brown pool of fear, deceit and misery.

One day, as she settled into the reality
that was now her ever changing home,
The seed, filled with goals, hopes and dreams
she had initially planted,
Shyly poked out of the ground.

She stopped and stared in disbelief
At the budding of the magical bean,
Looked up to the sky,
And welcomed her blessings.

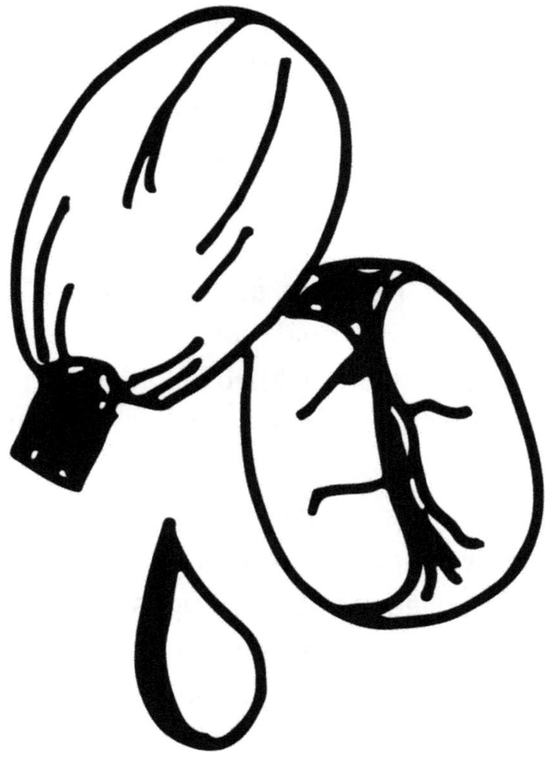

'Coffea tree'

I urge you to be as wise
As the African coffea tree
Keeping in mind that sometimes the people around you
Will not support you in the way you deserve.

Work in silence to become stronger and
Be ready when harvest season arrives
For it is when you will see the fruits of your labour
Successfully shedding its final morsels of negativity, and
Painlessly gaining access to
That bittersweet bean of life.

Crush it.

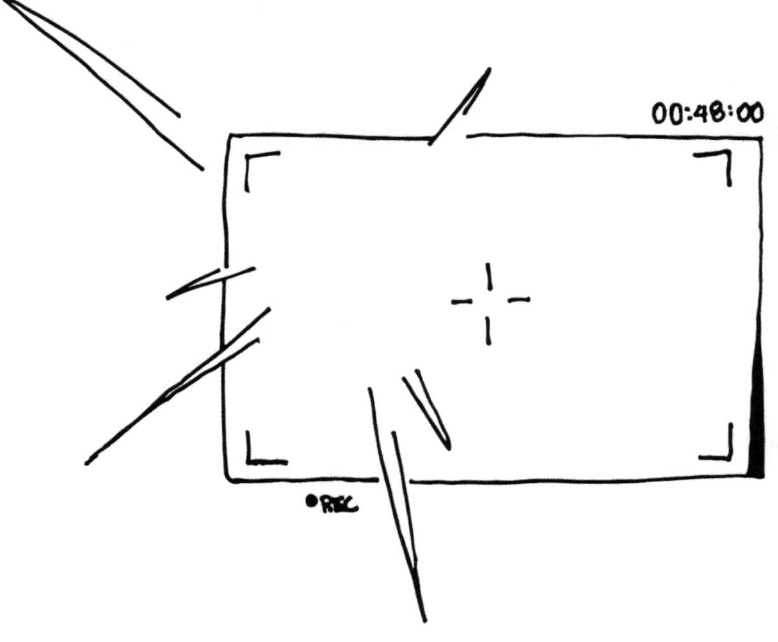

00:48:00
● REC

'Brightness'

She held nothing back—
Not her thoughts or her dreams,
Nor her inquisitiveness or her schemes.
She was loud, proud and everything in between, and
Didn't care about fitting into any type of scene.

They always called that girl ruthless, but
She was only fearlessly expressing her brightness.

Aissatou Bah

'Motherland'

A world enriched with
Much of earth's most valuable resources
Never existed
Until Africaland was created.

Its very soil,
Cultivated and nourished
By strong Black hands blessed by the Lord.

'Knowledge'

She held the Book of Life in her hands,
Taking great care not to rush through its story
As she flipped through its leaves.

Admiring the tiny thought patterns
Leading into its spine, and
Embracing its imperfections, taught her
The utmost important lesson in patience.

At the end of the tale,
As she turned to the last page—
The synopsis reflected an ancient's
Conventional story on its way to becoming history . . .

'Mistakes'

Remaining tied down by your past mistakes
Is an invitation to drown

'Bridges'

Turn these tears into lessons,
Turn these lessons into blessings,
Turn these blessings into bridges,
And these bridges?
Into poems.

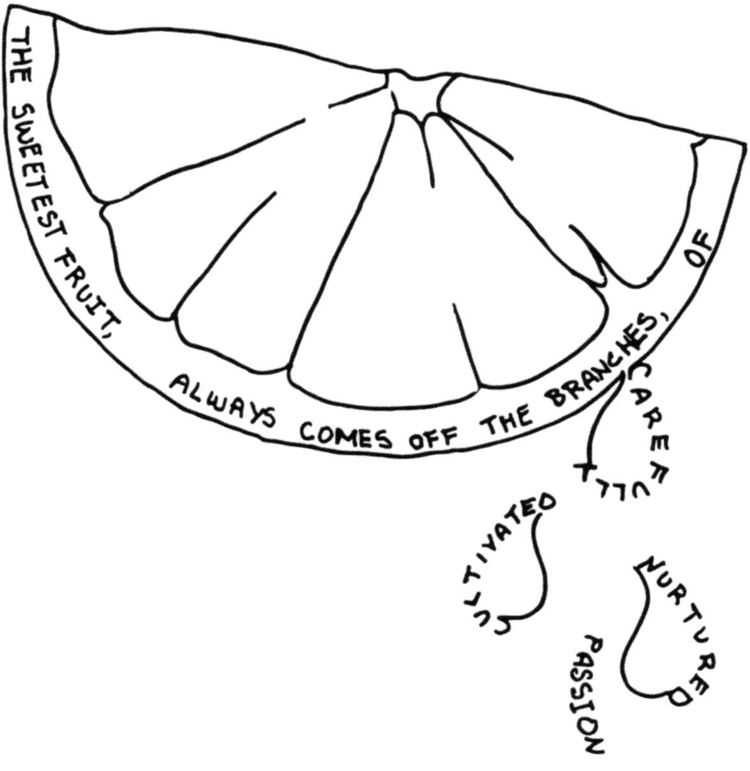
THE SWEETEST FRUIT, ALWAYS COMES OFF THE BRANCHES, OF
CAREFULLY
CULTIVATED
NURTURED
PASSION

'Passionfruit'

The sweetest fruit
Always falls off the branches
Of carefully cultivated, and
Nurtured passion.

Aissatou Bah

'Cherries'

Tell them to leave you alone if
They plan on interfering with
The growth of your cherry tree.
Its branches may not always be strong,
Especially when negativity is blown your way, but,

In spite of occasional strong winds,
Your cherries shall continue to grow—
Seasonally.

Aissatou Bah

'Sunflowers'

I wish that people were as wholly, as a
Field blooming with sunflowers are to the sun.

'Thirst'

I plucked a sunflower, using my thumb and index and,
Observed as her seeds sprang into formation.

Much to my surprise,
They effortlessly created a line of loyal soldiers,
Eager to quench a thirst
That could only be satisfied by the sun.

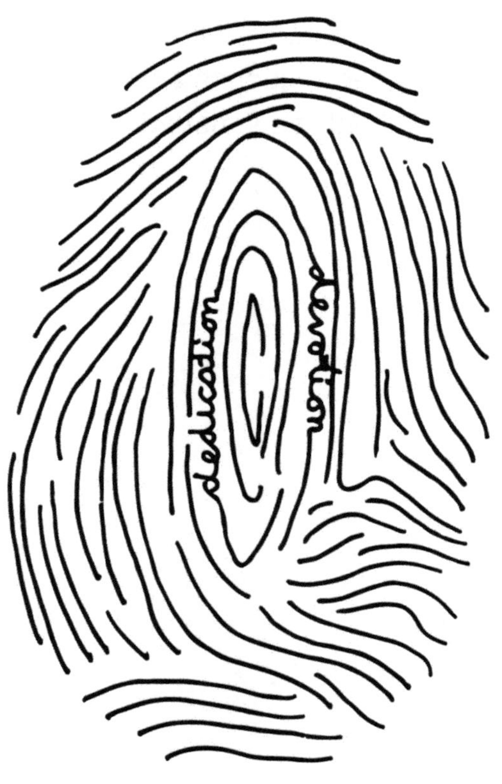

dedication
devotion

'Soulmates'

Maybe your soulmate is actually
The dedication imprisoned in your mind,
Trying to reach
The untapped devotion in your fingers.

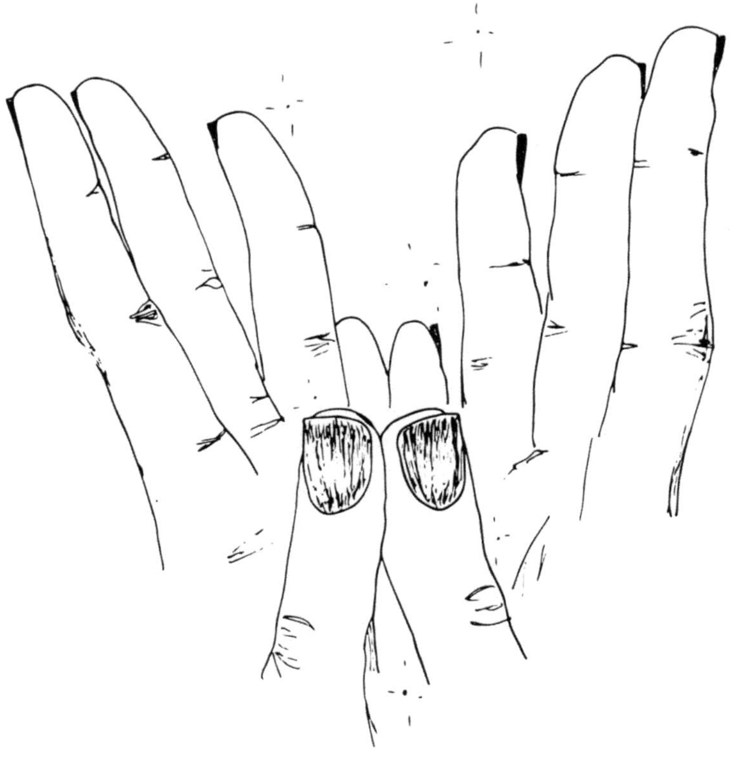

'Glory'

Give thanks to your palms.
They're the ones who press confidence within, and
Allow your glory to unfold.

'July 12'

It was a particularly cool summer's day on July 12 when she emerged into the world. Soft cries followed a moment of silence. Warm hugs followed tears of joy. It took years for her to experience life-changing growth. Yesterday, she was small and wild; but today, she's tall and mild. Her strong mind and equally tough limbs are proof of resilient African roots. To her, summer is not a season, but is in fact a home. It's the select moments where she can let her hair down and allow her stretch-mark printed belly to see the light. It is where her unique and timeless experiences matter the most. Her best memories almost always involve sunshine. As we speak, she's out there dancing in a blue ocean, surrounded by a fragrant floral breeze, and consistently welcoming the sun's love.

ROYALTY

'The King'

He stood before me,
Grabbing hold of my hand,
When the villagers around us,
Could not be bothered to take a stand.

He defended me,
With no fear or hesitance,
Obstructing the harsh slurs,
Directed at me by the peasants.

He ensured I was safe,
Guiding me to my home,
And upon entering, my mother noticed
where tears not long ago laid.
She inquired of the events, settling quietly on her throne.
Taking a deep breath I said, "A young Black man
came to my aid."

I recounted my tale, without missing a beat.
At the end of my speech, my mother smiled and stood,
Gesturing for me to rise on my feet,
She finally spoke; "This man is a blessing and did you good,"
Do not cry, sweet child of mine, nor forget this day,
As this man has his own dragons to slay.
For he is a King, as brave as they come,
Suffering silently in his own Kingdom."

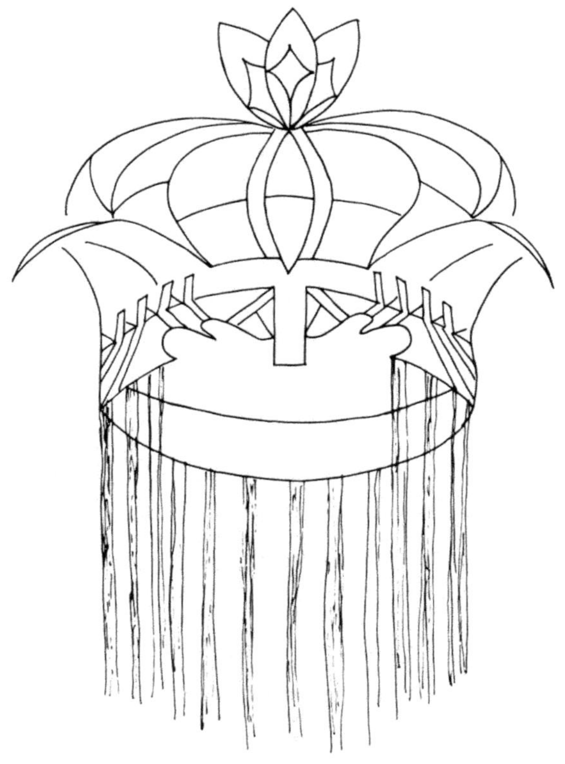

'Father'

He learned what patience meant
Once he had not one,
Not two, but three daughters.

What he thought were turbulent phases,
Emerged as ambition.
What he believed was anger,
Turned out to be passion.

The previous rules once taught by his successors
Were shattered by three beautiful princesses
Who had successfully made him King.

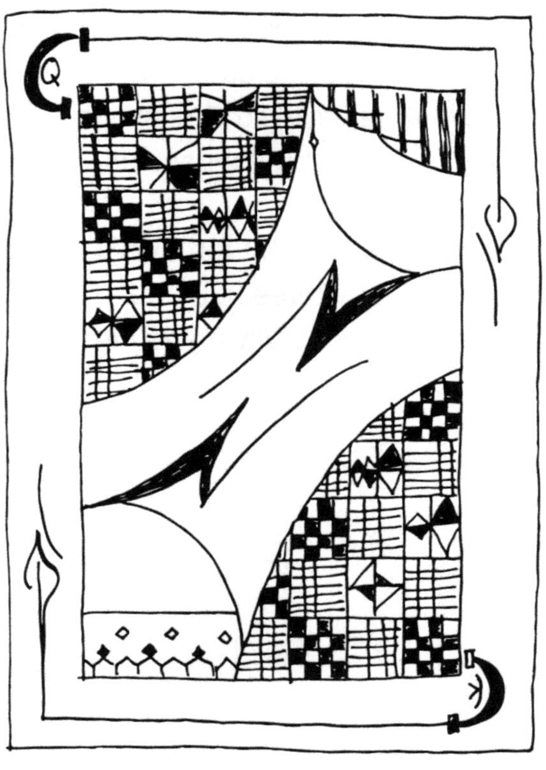

'Castle'

A castle is nothing without a King.

A King is nothing without a Queen.

A Queen is *everything*
When a community supports her.

Aissatou Bah

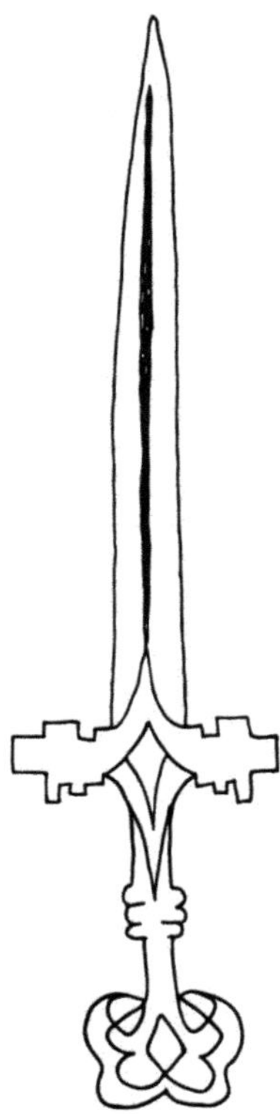

'Burning Tower'

I used to think that you were the key—
That you'd save me from the summit of my burning tower.
But you're just a trap.
And I am *finally* ready to defend myself from your attack.

'Fierce'

Even the fiercest dragon
Cannot keep warm without exhaling.

Aissatou Bah

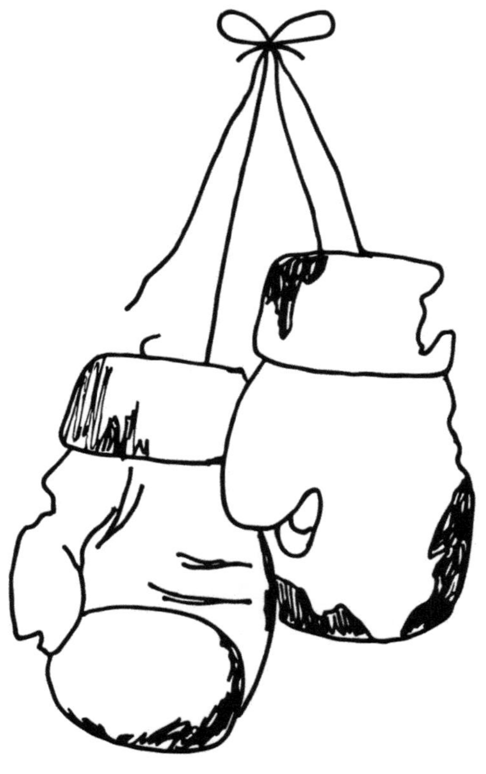

'Firefighter'

I want you to look at this burned down place, and see it as
A reminder that even though you failed,
At least you fought fire.

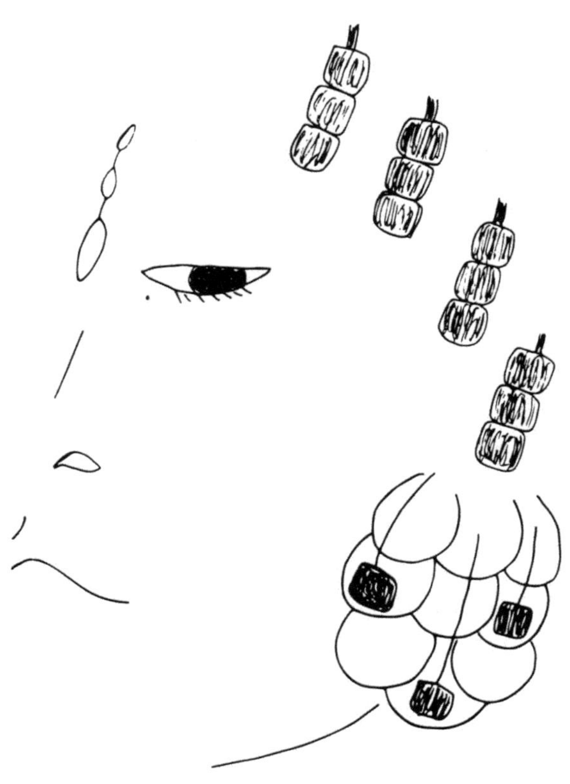

'The Queen'

She glides into her castle
Leaving gold dust in her wake,
Observing the people who doubted her
Crumble to the realization that
They dished out *much more* than they could take.

Aissatou Bah

'Reign'

No matter how hard they try to reign on your parade,
Never accept defeat.

'Le Chemin du Roi'

The road to the Kingdom
Looks eerily bleak
If you carelessly kick pebbles around,
Without taking proper aim.

'Pebble'

Throw a pebble
At the bottom of a well
And watch it sink
Into the dark depths
Of uncertainty.

Then, darling, practice patience.
Because if you wait long enough,
The pebble meets a rock at the bottom—

Everything plinks.

Aissatou Bah

'Tick Tock'

I am the tic,
Lurking in your clock,
Seizing every opportunity to approach you—
Like a moth closing in on a flame.

I am the toc,
The sound of murmurs around town,
Where everyone lurks, eyes wide open,
As you prepare to grab ahold of your crown.

FROM WITHIN

Aissatou Bah

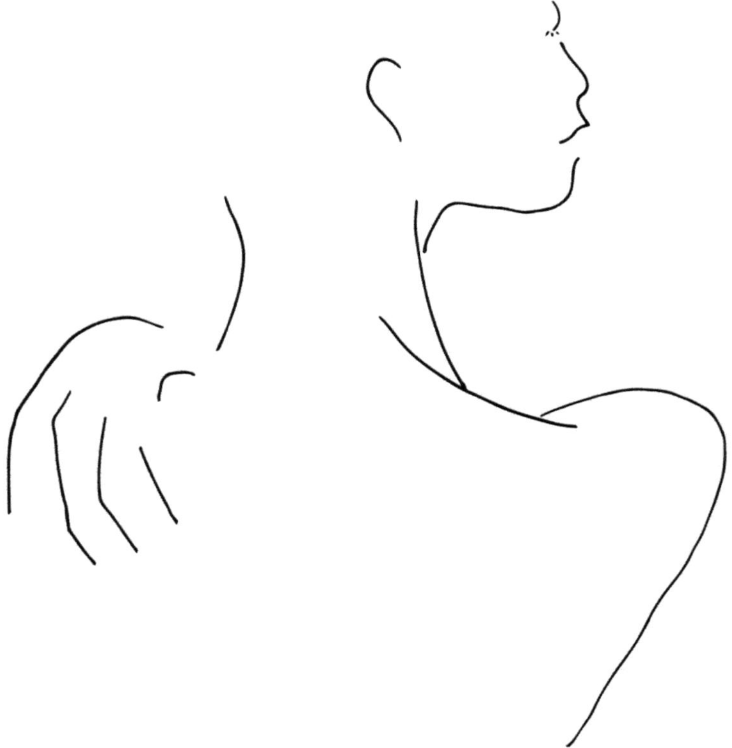

'Self Love'

Today I have decided
I'll start with loving me:

L will be for letting go of the self-doubt
O for owning the truth in my route
V can be for adopting a valiant temper
While E is everything I know I have the courage to be
M for the moments that taught me the most, and
The final E shall be for kissing all enemies *goodbye*.

Aissatou Bah

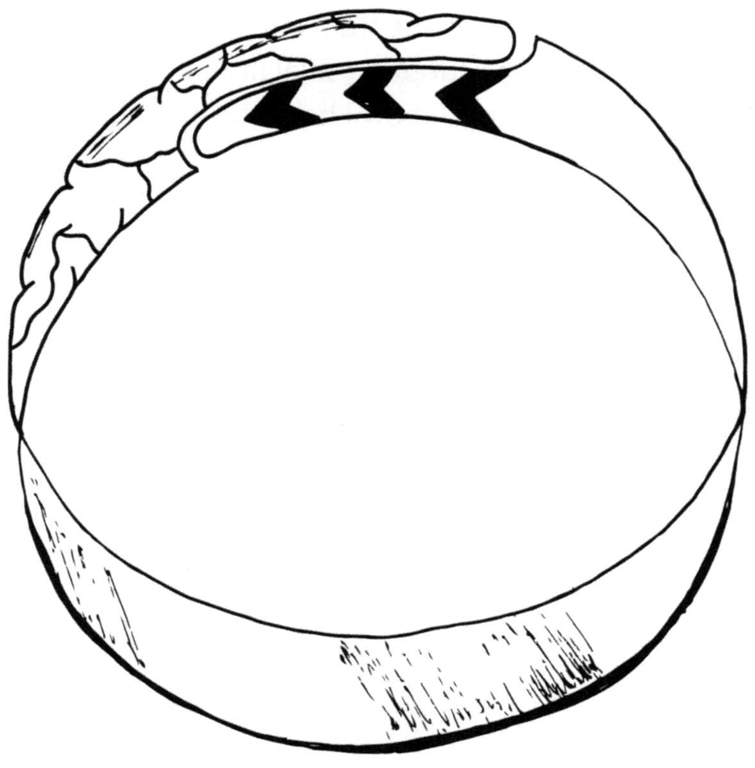

'Alternative Vows'

"Dearly beloved, we are gathered here today to join this cerebrum and this purpose in (holy) matrimony. Cerebrum, do you take this woman to be your priority, to live together in (holy) matrimony, to love and honour her, to comfort her, and to keep her in sickness and in health, forsaking all others, for as long as you shall live?"

"I do."

*"Purpose, do you take this woman
to make use of your hands, to live
together in harmony, to drive her, push her to her limits,
to inspire her, and to keep
her curious and determined, for as long as you shall live?"*

"I do."

"You may now go forth and fulfill your vows with the same love and devotion, that now blossoms between you."

Aissatou Bah

'Directions'

The path you decide to journey on,
Most certainly, splits into multiple directions.

Wander aimlessly.

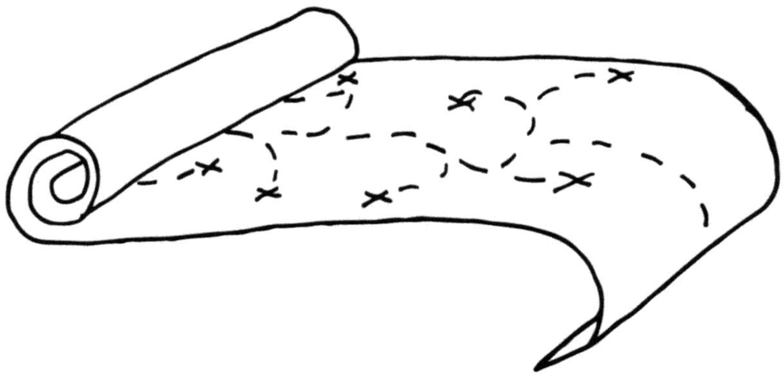

'Wanderlust Girl'

She is a strange wanderlust girl—
Afraid to wander, but excited to wonder.

Exploring several villages, one after the other,
She experiences tidbits of the world, and finally decides
She wants to continue experiencing her quest
to self-discovery.

Aissatou Bah

'Enough'

There's a beast out there—
Someone telling you that you are not enough.

Dismiss these lies—
Replacing the mold on your rock,
With abundant patches of moss.

Even when you believe all is covered,
Don't be satisfied until you're equipped with
More than enough.

Aissatou Bah

'Stardust'

Break free from the centre
Of this destructive tornado, and
Become your own explosive stardust.

'Night Wails'

You've been talking in your sleep—
Revealing everything you can't
While you're conscious and tend to weep.
After you've drained yourself with all of the sad songs,
It's only be a matter of time
Until your night wails turn into the best of dreams.

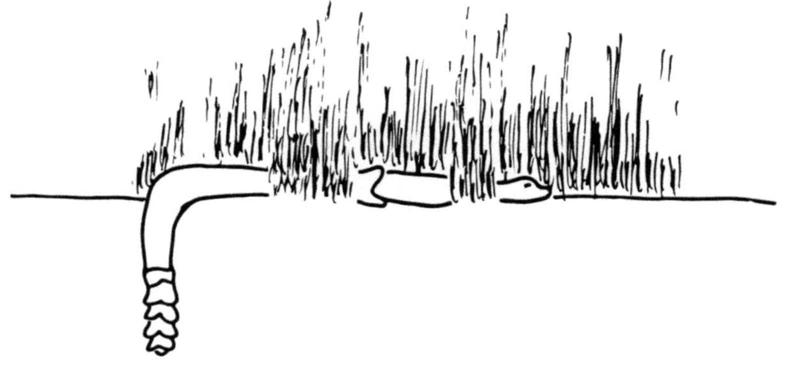

'Rooted'

One day we're inseparable, and
The other . . . I don't even recognize you.

You've hidden yourself somewhere in the garden.

You've left me behind, like a snake shedding its skin.
All is not well, but
I can't wait to measure your growth once you've rooted.

'Butterfly'

The world is a garden of sunflowers,
Daisies, weeds, and all kinds of wildflowers.
As you bloom, remember to
Proudly flutter those distinctly unique wings—
A testimony of the difficult transitions you overcame,
Just to be able to brush the air
In soft, confident strokes.

we are made
of
sunlight
and
love

'Daisies'

Like daisies,
We are made out of sunlight and love.

Aissatou Bah

'Wilt'

I shall cry, grow, wilt and repeat.

I shall repeat, wilt, grow and cry.

Pieces of me will vanish,
but I shall always remain and rebuild.

Aissatou Bah

'Someone'

I want someone to look at me like I'm a rainbow; full of colours and essentially, a child of the sun. But I also want that person to understand why I sometimes hide behind the clouds, disappearing for days at a time and standing underneath the rain during a storm. And then, I want her to hear the sound of butterflies fluttering their wings and busy bees collecting nectar. I want her to dare me to touch the wind, encouraging it to kiss my pain away. I want that girl to remind me that **I am beautiful** and **powerful** and **intuitive** and **gifted** and **absolutely worthy** of existing.

I *want* that woman to be me.

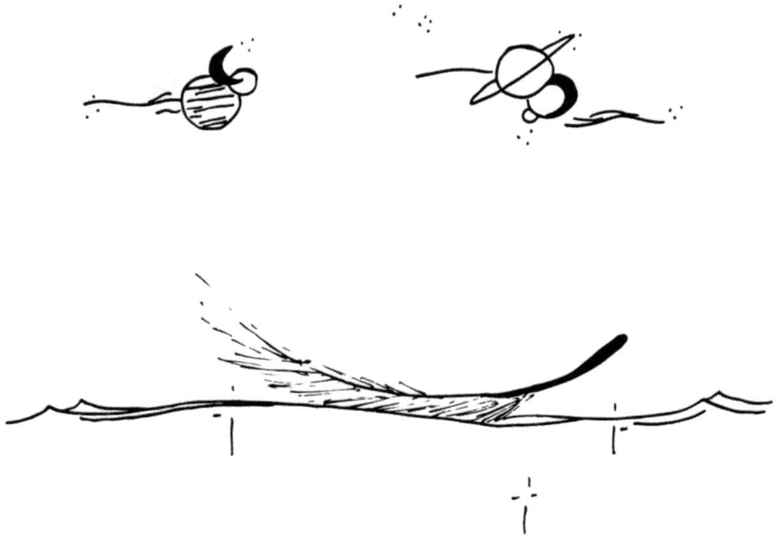

'High'

I'd like to fall in love someday and be
Surrounded by a million stars and a dozen planets.

I'd like to be high
Staring down onto a black and empty ocean.

I'd like to descend softly onto it, like a feather,
Reaching an unprecedented level of peace.

I'd like to lift my index to touch the gleaming
creature on its surface
Eventually smiling at the stunning reflection of me.

'Memories'

You remind me of a garden
A complex ecosystem
Neutralized by an earthy melanin soil,
Hundreds of floral seeds, and
Select pesky weeds.

Those of which, are all proof of the true and powerful
Existence of a happy heart full of infinite memories.

Aissatou Bah

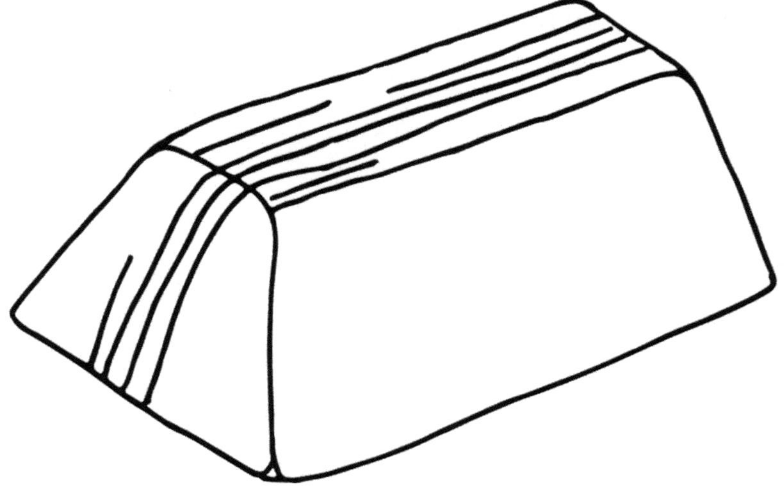

'Rainbow'

Be the pot of gold
At the extremity of your rainbow.

Aissatou Bah

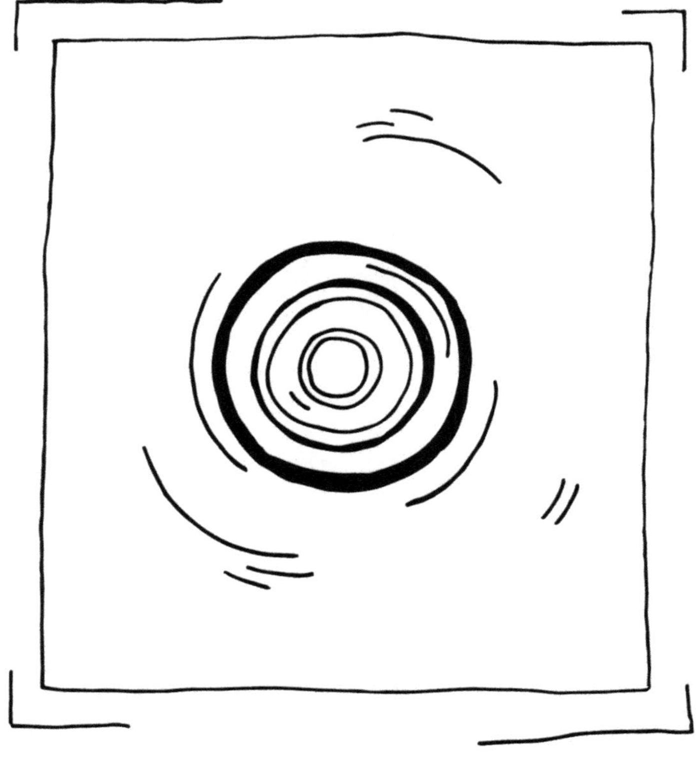

'Vibrations'

Existing with a broken heart,
Will only pressure a decaying idea
To reverberate throughout your body—
Forcing a pulsating motion
To cause a collateral commotion
In your energy field.

Focus on the bigger picture.
Press refresh on your thoughts and
Create enough space to welcome brand-new vibrations.

PUSH & PULL

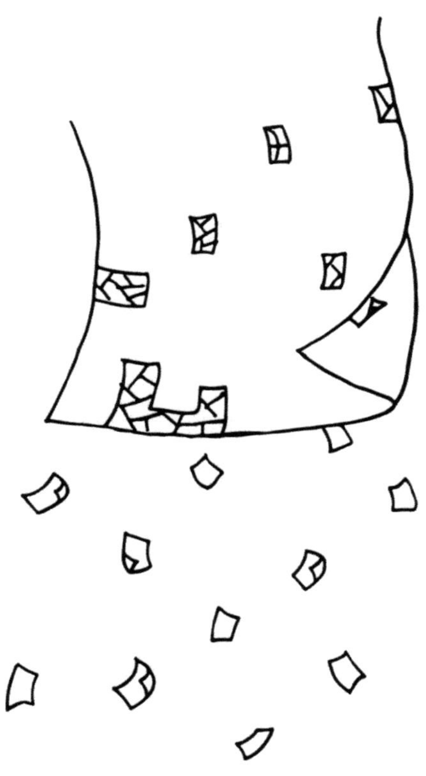

'Energy'

Life is energy—
Colourful pieces of flexible fabric
That multiplies itself, and
Explodes into never-ending confetti.

Aissatou Bah

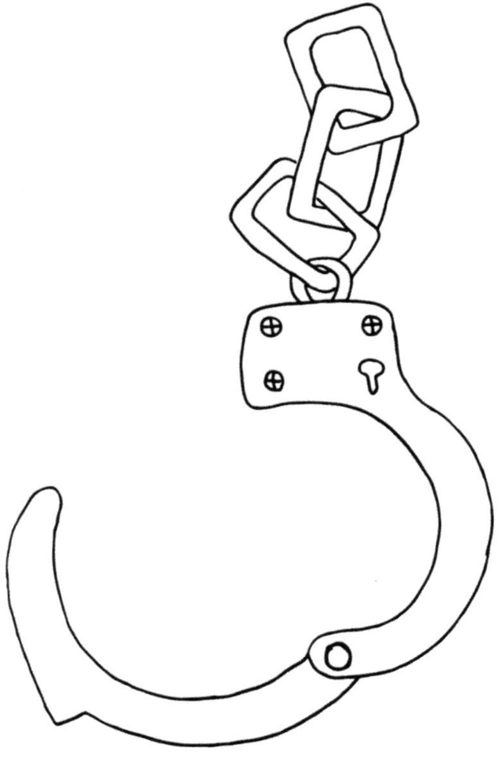

'Life'

Afraid to live,
Or afraid to die?

Surely, you are *breathing*.

Afraid to die,
Or afraid to live?

Surely, you are *free*.

'Sandwich'

Life is the best and worst tasting meal.
And ripping its endless lessons and mistakes apart
Is like ruining a perfectly edible sandwich.

Aissatou Bah

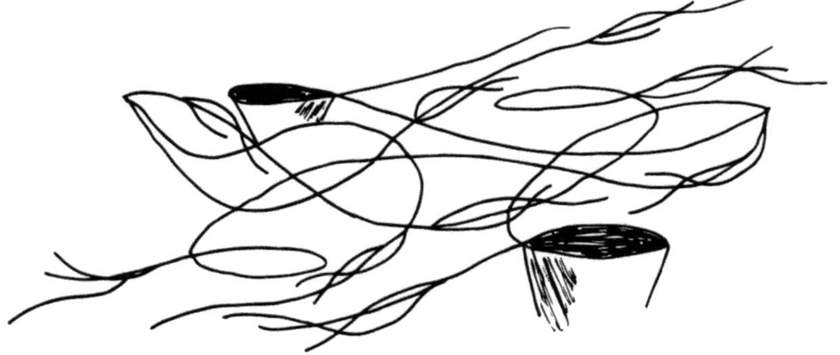

'Tangled'

Life is a tangled web
Weaved of tiny strands, but
Built stronger than the cables
That hold up the Golden Gate Bridge.

These lines sometimes lead to
Wisdom and grace,
Other times, driving us into
Plot holes and moments of solace.

While it's uncertain
How long this cycle will last,
The safety of your net
Is entirely dependent
On the foundations you lay.

'Moongrave'

There's a graveyard on the moon
Where doubt and fear are buried—
Invisible one day and prominent the next,
Shedding light on what is real and what is a hoax.

A single touch of reality
Can illuminate the heart's true mate,
Moving forward on its silver surface,
Where darkness, eventually meets fate.

Nothing can stop the time in which your phase will begin,
But you can choose to gravitate
Away from what lurks in the shadows—

Leave the bones behind you, and
Create a path adorned with
New and improved sets of footprints.

Aissatou Bah

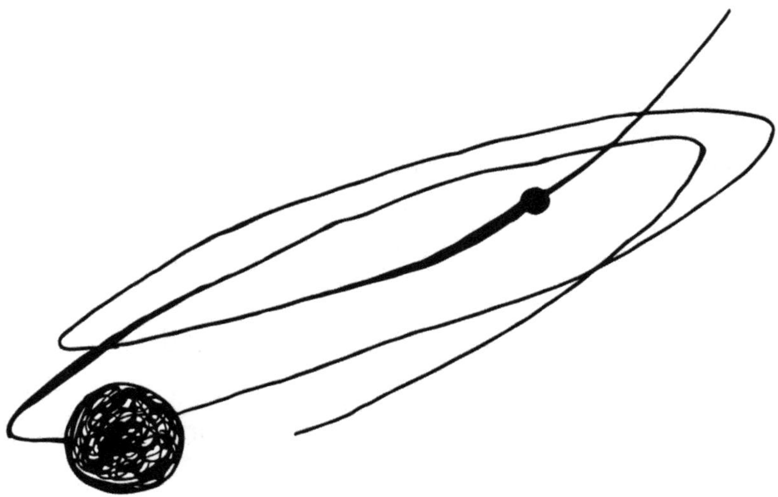

176

'Catch'

In time, the sun's uncomfortable warmth
Will catch up with the icy moon.

Aissatou Bah

'Eclipse'

In the face of an eclipsed moon,
You shall be the light.

Take up all the space
You need to fill in the
————————,
But predestined purpose
In your creed.

'Space'

Take up all the space you need to
Fill in the blank, but predestined purpose in your creed.

Aissatou Bah

'Cosmic Highway'

Stride to the beat of the earth's vibrations.
Heal its cracked roads with your movements,
Seal its potholes with fragrant bouquets,
Expand and spiral within its cosmic heart and—
Arrive at your final destination, at the end of the highway.

Aissatou Bah

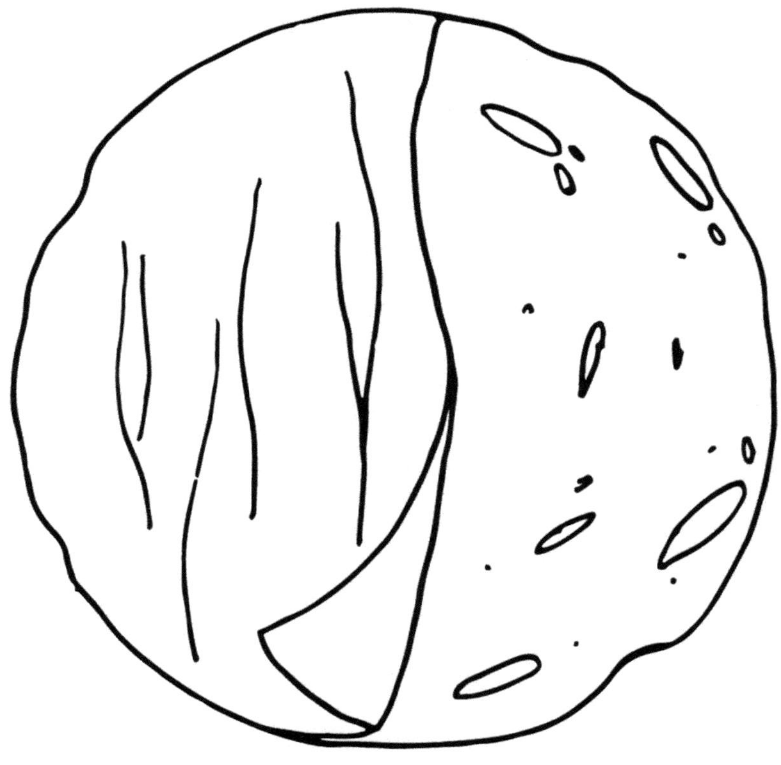

'Sing'

When you left,
The moon became angry at us;
Its shell turning into an impenetrable husk.

So I sang to her,
Making sure she knew I appreciated her light—
And she eventually stopped putting up a fight.

'The Key'

The key to opening the doors to love and light
Is realizing that you are both the object and the enabler.

Holding one key guarantees entrance to a single door
But holding multiple, grants access to a garden.

Aissatou Bah

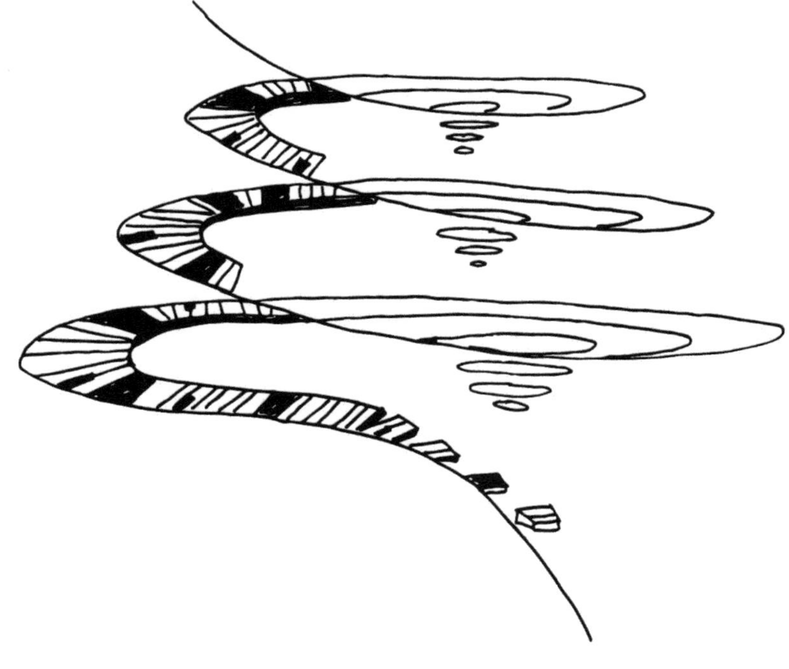

'Dream'

If life isn't an endless dream,
Then I want you to capture these precious moments,
Trap them into the keys of a piano,
And play the softest, sweetest melody leading into
our closing credits . . .

'Blessed'

I wake up lucky
Positively blessed
God has raised me
In the middle of my mess
So, I fall, then stand
Finding the courage
To smile with my teeth
To smell the rain
And to dance in the sun
Because I wake up
Lucky
Positively blessed.

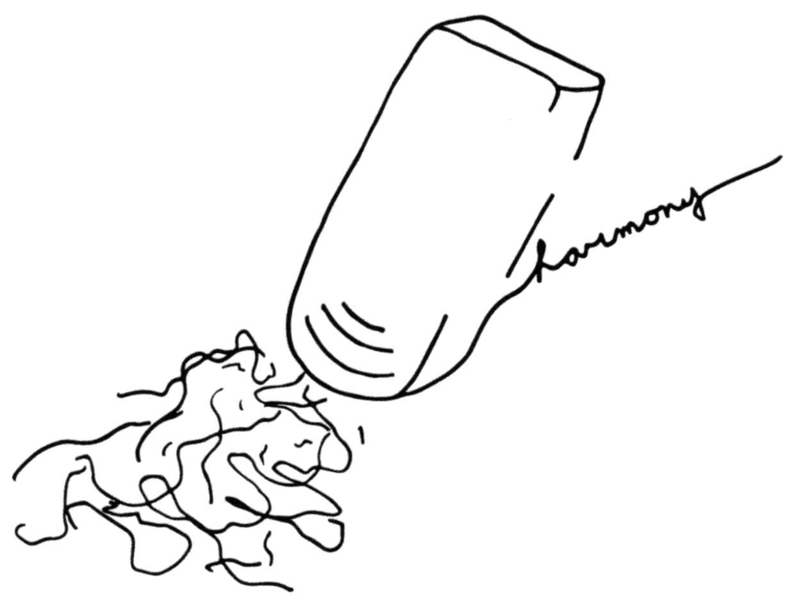

The four elements of Ho'oponopono: I'm sorry (repentance), please forgive me (ask), thank you (gratitude) and I love you (love).

'Ho'oponopono'

There exists an ancient meditation originating from the Hawaiian Islands, stipulating that in order to experience harmony we must take responsibility of all pain—including that of which we indirectly cause. More often than not, the errors we find in others can also be found in us. Decidedly, it's essential to focus and rectify all troubling events that occur today *(kala)* and yesterday*('oki)*—not tomorrow.

Owning your truth means pushing the ego aside and accepting responsibility while still moving forward in life. When that shift occurs, you gain a sense of control that energizes your psyche. Erase the preconceived ideas you have written about others in order to know yourself and appease the sufferance on both you and your community. By doing so, we effectively implement reconciliation and forgiveness towards the ones we love—especially family.

With that being said, I'd like to start replacing my 'I'm sorry ifs' to 'I'm sorry that' and my 'It's not my faults' to reflecting in silence. Allowing clarity and positivity to enter. This will only feel like a bumpy road if pride is at the wheel. However, it turns into a smooth one once negativity is dissolved and promptly replaced by light. Restoring faith, love and empathy in humanity only begins when it truly resonates from within.

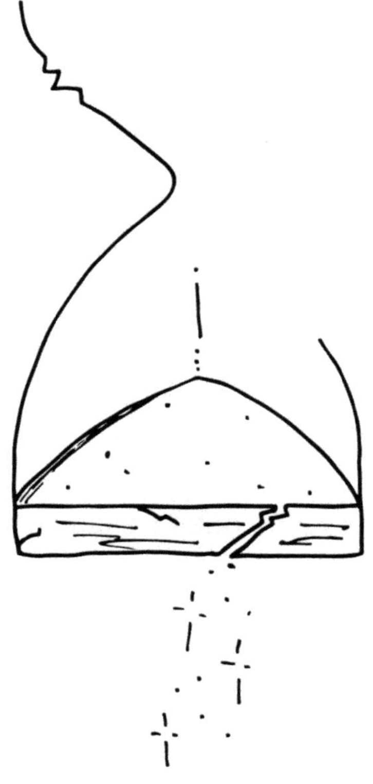

'Star Power'

After every speck of sand has reached
the bottom of the hourglass, and
Every shard has been filtered as the seconds pass,
A lightning bolt shall light the sky—
Warning you that it is time
To share your star power.

Aissatou Bah

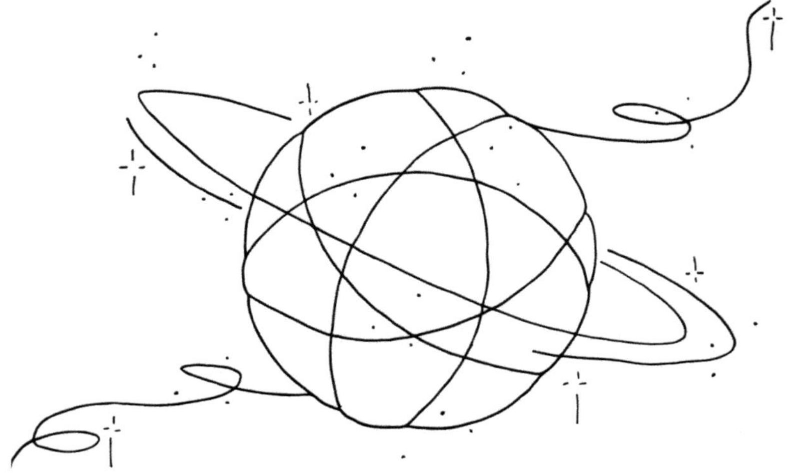

'A Beautiful Collision'

Our love maps are etched from the same stardust.
Tugging from one corner, rolls us into one—
Creating a beautiful collision
That encompasses all of the stars and planets
Keeping us apart from one another.

Aissatou Bah

'Syzygy'

You are the moon—
I am the sun.

Together, waltzing on this earth,
We form a beautiful syzygy.

Aissatou Bah

'Art'

Art is the pearl
Visible at dawn
And gone at dusk.

Art is moonlight—
Shadow to crater,
Pinky to crust.

Art is a wound.
Art is the dust.
But most importantly,
Art is you—
Art is *us*.

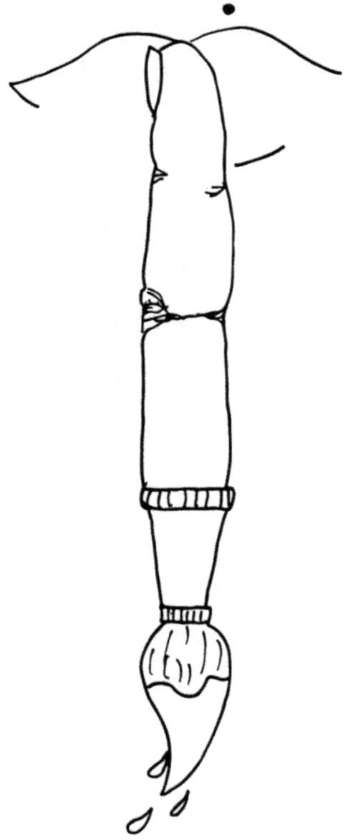

'Words'

When words fail,
Art prevails.

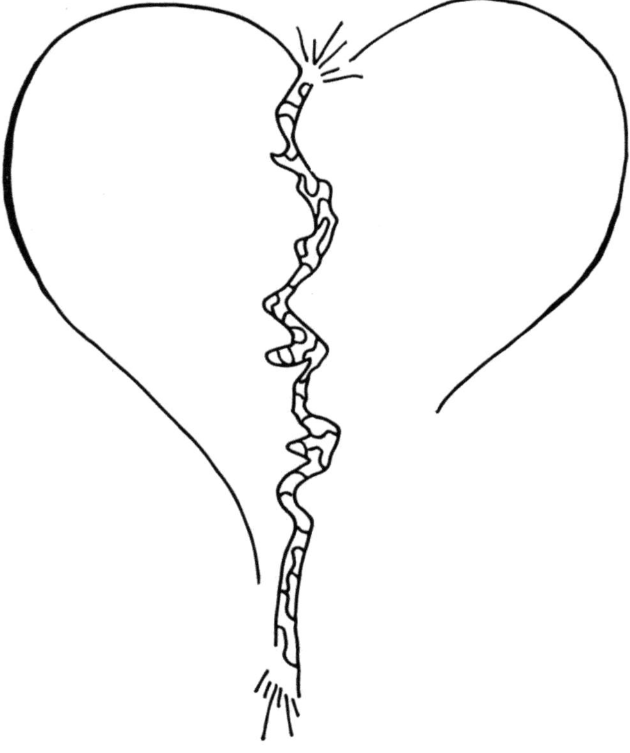

'Fusion'

If fused fragments make a whole,
Then surely, your broken heart shall mend.

Aissatou Bah

'Thrive'

They don't appreciate the true value of the shy girls
Because of the discomfort that is always felt
in their silent world.

The truth is, we understand its stillness,
Choosing to only thrive in the presence of ones
who are worthy.

'Storm'

Even in the wildest of storms,
Have the courage to see past the clouds
And embrace the lightning.

Aissatou Bah

'Flood'

What began as a few raindrops,
Turned into a raging flood—
One that tried to damage her heart, but instead,
Filled it with more empathy than she's ever known.

'Valuable'

You may have been broken a million times
In a billion types of ways

You may have been used
So much so, that you rarely recognize love

You may have cried tears
Enough to cover earth's water supply twice over.

But Queen, never forget,
That even if you are 'damaged' goods
You are still valuable goods.

Cherished.

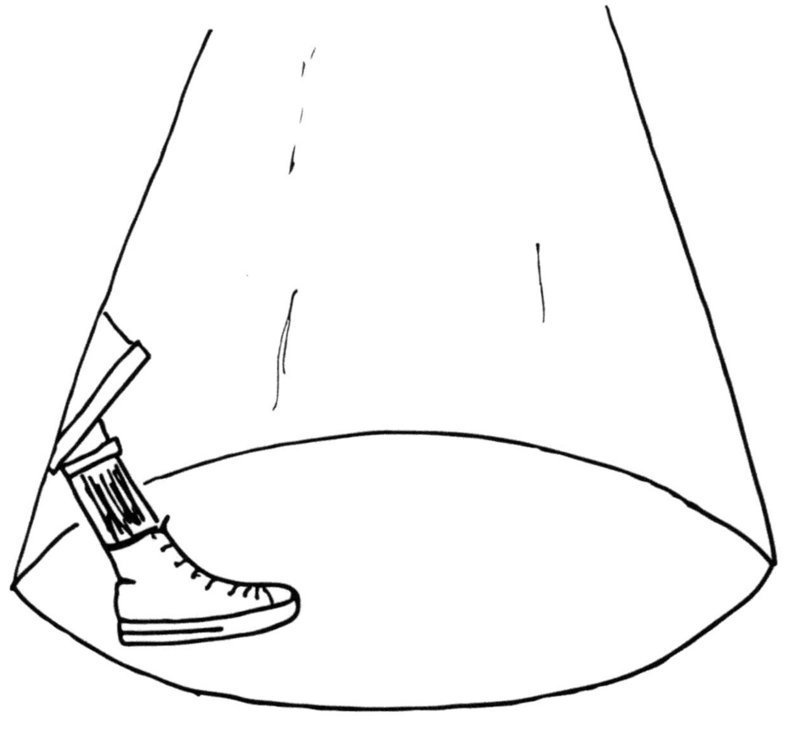

'A Million Reasons'

There are probably a million reasons you could list to
Try and convince me that you should quit, but
There is, but only one, single reason
That should make you want to stay:

The world is ready for you.

Lightning Source UK Ltd.
Milton Keynes UK
UKHW020658011020
370849UK00009B/257